COLORS
IN BLOOM

Use color to create 21 silk flower
arrangements for every mood and décor

Terry L. Rye

NORTH LIGHT BOOKS
CINCINNATI, OHIO
www.artistsnetwork.com

ABOUT THE AUTHOR

Terry Rye has a passion for flowers and the best job in the world—creating exceptionally beautiful floral designs. Since 1980, she has owned The Mariemont Florist in Cincinnati, Ohio. Highly regarded as a distinguished professional florist, The Mariemont Florist has been featured in numerous floral publications and in the prestigious Cincinnati Flower Show. As a self-taught floral designer, Terry loves to share the joy of flower arranging with others through her series of floral how-to books and as a presenter on the DIY Network, which is part of the HGTV family. She has also been featured in many special interest segments locally as well as nationally. Terry resides in Cincinnati, Ohio, with her husband, Doug Eisele, and daughters, Trina and Sarah.

Colors in Bloom. Copyright © 2004 by Terry L. Rye. Manufactured in China. All rights reserved. No part of this book may be reproduced in any form or by any electronic or mechanical means including information storage and retrieval systems without permission in writing from the publisher, except by a reviewer who may quote brief passages in a review. Published by North Light Books, an imprint of F&W Publications, Inc., 4700 East Galbraith Road, Cincinnati, Ohio, 45236. (800) 289-0963. First Edition.

Other fine North Light Books are available from your local bookstore, art supply store or direct from the publisher.

08 07 06 05 04   5 4 3 2 1

Library of Congress Cataloging-in-Publication Data
Rye, Terry L.
    Colors in bloom : use color to create 21 silk flower arrangements for
    every mood and décor / Terry L. Rye.
        p. cm
    Includes index.
    ISBN 1-58180-556-X (pbk. : alk. paper)
    1. Silk flower arrangement. I. Title.

SB449.3.S44R935 2003
745.92—dc22

2003064959

Edited by Amanda Metcalf
Interior designed by Lisa Buchanan
Cover designed by Stephanie Strang
Production art by Karla Baker
Production coordinated by Sara Dumford
Photographs by Christine Polomsky and Al Parrish
Photo styling by Jan Nickum

METRIC CONVERSION CHART

To convert	to	multiply by
Inches	Centimeters	2.54
Centimeters	Inches	0.4
Feet	Centimeters	30.5
Centimeters	Feet	0.03
Yards	Meters	0.9
Meters	Yards	1.1
Sq. Inches	Sq. Centimeters	6.45
Sq. Centimeters	Sq. Inches	0.16
Sq. Feet	Sq. Meters	0.09
Sq. Meters	Sq. Feet	10.8
Sq. Yards	Sq. Meters	0.8
Sq. Meters	Sq. Yards	1.2
Pounds	Kilograms	0.45
Kilograms	Pounds	2.2
Ounces	Grams	28.3
Grams	Ounces	0.035

ACKNOWLEDGMENTS

Many thanks to all the talented people at The Mariemont Florist for their support and dedication during the completion of this book and for their contributions.

As always, I am grateful to be working with such an experienced, helpful and fun group of individuals from F+W Publications. They are so instrumental in making my series of books a tremendous success. With their attention to detail, my editors, Catherine Cochran and Amanda Metcalf, did a wonderful job in picking up the loose ends when I needed it. Christine Polomsky has a keen ability to conceptualize photos that are clear and easy to understand. She makes the written step-by-step instructions come alive through her photography. My heartfelt thanks always go to Tricia Waddell, who has continued to believe in my creative abilities for great how-to books. And many thanks to all the other wonderful people behind the scenes that edit, compile, proofread, produce and sell the books.

I want to also thank all the talented and creative people that have purchased my books and have made their own arrangements with a little help from me. These books would not be possible without you!

I am truly blessed with a talented staff, a great publisher, wonderful friends and an incredibly supportive, loving family—Doug, Trina and Sarah—who never let me lose sight of what is truly important in life—loved ones.

DEDICATION

With much love and appreciation, I dedicate this book to my husband, Doug Eisele, and my daughters, Trina and Sarah, for their support, understanding and continuous enthusiasm for my work as a floral author.

Contents

1 Warm Colors {page 14}

Make a bold statement with these arrangements, whether you want cozy, romantic or dramatic. Add a punch of color to a neutral room or bring the colors of a room together.

2 Cool Colors {page 40}

Cool can be snazzy, calming or energizing like a splash of cold water. Whether you want to add a personal touch to a relaxing room or wow guests with a splashy, flashy arrangement, you'll find what you need right here.

3 Pastels {*page 58*}

Add a soft touch to any room to match the mood or season. Pastels use muted, unimposing colors that are inviting and soothing, incorporating cute whimsy or soft elegance.

4 Neutrals {*page 88*}

Neutrals complement so many colors, rooms and moods. They imitate nature, and their impact comes not from the colors themselves but from how they are put together. Combined, these flowers and foliage offer so much beauty.

5 Shades of Black & White {*page 110*}

Black-and-white arrangements are appealing in the way they complement each other and other colors. They bespeak simplicity and drama, vintage appeal and contemporary flair all at once. See what you can make of these unexpected hues.

Introduction

Color sets the mood, in you and in your home. So it's the most important element in any flower arrangement. Setting the right mood is all about finding the colors that most appeal to you.

Identify the colors that you are drawn to, the ones that draw you in. Whether you've meant to or not, you've probably already chosen "your colors" in your decorating. People love to use color in fabric, furniture, wall coverings and decorative accents to create environments in which they feel comfortable.

Let the vivid colors created by flowers add to the atmosphere you've already created in your home. Silk flowers allow you to design arrangements all year round that fit you and your décor, and they'll look beautiful for a long time so you can enjoy them as long as you want.

Look through this book and focus on the feelings each arrangement creates within you. Study the colors and how they work together. Which colors make you feel calm? Which colors give a sense of energy and clarity? What moods do you want to convey in certain rooms?

Warm colors can be cozy and comforting or they can be dramatic and romantic. Cool shades can help you relax or make you feel refreshed—great shades to help you cool off on a warm day!

Pastels are understated versions of warm and cool colors. They're soft and muted and can create the coziness of warm flowers and the relaxing setting of cool flowers. Put them in a quiet room where you go to escape the rush and flurry of day-to-day life. Neutral arrangements can blend into the background or make a bold statement with size, shape and design. And arrangements of black, white and gray add a contemporary zest.

In the following chapters, you'll find centerpiece, candleholder, topiary and vase arrangements, using fruit, vegetables, foliage and a wide array of silk flowers. You'll also discover plenty of fun and easy techniques to make your containers and arrangements fit your décor. So let the colors of nature inspire you, and start arranging today!

Getting Ready to Arrange

Before you start inserting flowers into foam, there's just a bit of preparation to be done. Acquaint yourself with the tools and materials on this page and follow the steps to prepare your container and flowers for arranging.

BASIC SILK FLORAL TOOLS AND MATERIALS

1. Styrofoam comes in 2" (5cm) thick sheets and other shapes.
2. Foam blocks; glue bricks and blocks together to create a shape that fits your container.
3. Foam disks; some come with an adhesive patch on the bottom.
4. Paring knife to trim and cut foam.
5. Sand to weigh down a container or add a decorative touch.
6. Moss to cover foam.
7. Tape measure to measure stems.
8. Wire cutter to cut stems.
9. Hot glue gun and glue sticks for gluing foam, moss and embellishments.
10. Floral adhesive for securing candles and embellishments to foam.
11. Wooden floral picks to secure embellishments, such as faux fruit, in foam.
12. Greening pins for securing moss to foam.
13. Floral wire to help secure elements together in an arrangement.
14. Chenille stems for holding bouquets together.
15. Embellishments, such as candles and candleholders or faux fruit.
16. Foam glue for adhering Styrofoam to your container.

1 CUT AT THE NOTCHES ...

At the beginning of each project in this book, I've listed the length to cut each stem. It's easier and safer to cut each stem at the closest notch to that length.

2 UNLESS THERE ARE NO NOTCHES ...

If the stem doesn't have notches or if it's really thick, cut as deeply as you can into the stem, twisting as you cut to get more leverage.

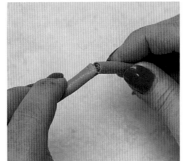

3 ... THEN BEND AND SNAP

Bend the stem back and forth until it breaks. If necessary, clean up the cut edge with wire cutters.

4 CLEAN IT UP

Once you've measured and cut the stem, also remove any foliage near the bottom so the stem will enter the foam easily.

5 SPREAD THE FOLIAGE

Slightly bend the tips of the leaves so they point downward. The leaves and blossoms don't have to be completely symmetrical. In fact, the stem will look more natural if the leaves aren't identical.

6 OPEN THE PETALS

Open the petals and adjust the petals and leaves so the flower looks natural. You can continue to make adjustments while you're arranging the flowers.

Creating Balance

Flower arranging is all about balance. That doesn't mean your arrangements have to be symmetrical. When you look at your arrangements, simply ask yourself, "Does this look balanced?" There are three ways to think about balance, whether designing or evaluating an arrangement: horizontal balance, vertical balance and color balance.

HORIZONTAL BALANCE

Unfortunately, balance isn't as simple as putting one flower on the left and one on the right. Design-wise, working in odd numbers—often threes—rather than even numbers creates a good design.

You might start an arrangement with one flower or bush in the middle. Next you might put a tall rose stem on the right. To work in odd numbers, you need to add two more roses. But you might be thinking, "If I add two roses on the left, the weight simply will shift to that side." Now you've got to start thinking beyond one dimension. Besides working side to side, you can control the height of your arrangement as well. One tall stem on the right can be balanced by two shorter stems on the left.

Creating Balance in All Directions

Although this arrangement simply looks full of bright, warm colors, there's more to it than that. The strongest color is the orange-red of these daisies. Notice I'm using an odd number (three) of these, and that they're balanced with one on either side and one in the middle. However, if each were set in the middle facing straight up, you wouldn't be able to see them except from above, so I've set the middle one at the back and the two side ones in the front.

Balancing Color

Each daisy is balanced by a flower of the same color. The result is a balanced arrangement that also features an interesting floral variety. Notice that I used short foliage as well as hanging blossoms to vertically balance the tight arrangement of flowers.

VERTICAL BALANCE

Similarly, you want to make sure your arrangement isn't top- or bottom-heavy for stability as well as aesthetic reasons. Even if you are working just in the center of an arrangement, balance one tall stem with two shorter ones. As you're working in vertical and horizontal balance, also change the angle at which you insert stems so that some blossoms face upwards and some face out. The amount of the blossom that you can see affects the balance, too.

If you've created what you think is a balanced arrangement, don't be tempted to add more blossoms to fill it out. You can use fillers such as foliage, whether entire stems or individual leaves, and baby's breath to bring it all together.

COLOR BALANCE

Just as you considered the height of the flowers when creating horizontal or vertical balance, also consider color. In other words, don't overload one side of an arrangement with a certain color. Just as height carries a certain visual weight, so do certain colors. You can easily imagine how black "weighs" more than white. More closely related to flower arranging, red would weigh more than yellow in equal amounts. If your color choices aren't balanced, your arrangement won't be either.

Balancing a Neutral Arrangement
Because colors in neutral arrangements are so similar, you won't have as much opportunity to use color to create balance or make a statement. In this case, I used height to create balance and drama. Six sarracenia lily stems provide the arrangement's height. Notice that, though all the stems are tall, each is set at a slightly different height. To balance this height but not take away from it, I added a stem of eucalyptus on each side.

Create Balance at Every Step
I made sure that each new element I added sat close to the Styrofoam ball so nothing would interfere with the balance and height I created in the picture at left. This arrangement forms a simple, balanced design while at the same time giving viewers so many interesting things to see once they look closer.

Using Color

Take a minute to study the color wheel on this page. Artists and designers use this chart to create color balance in their compositions. In flower arranging it isn't as important to exactly balance each component with its opposite. You can choose to create an entirely warm arrangement or a completely cool arrangement, for example. Or you can pull from all sides of the wheel to create a bright, cheerful arrangement. Still, this wheel can guide you when trying to create an arrangement with a certain feel or for a certain décor.

WARM AND COOL COLORS

Warm colors include yellow, yellow-orange, orange, red-orange and red. If you want a warm, cozy or romantic arrangement, these are the colors to pick from. Cool colors include violet, blue-violet, blue, blue-green and green. These colors lend a feeling of freshness and calm to a setting.

THE EXCEPTIONS

Yellow-green and red-violet are the deal-breakers. They ride the line between warm and cool colors and can become a source of confusion. Yellow-green, for example, will be warm if it leans closer to yellow and will be cool if it leans closer to pure green. Red-violet will become warmer the closer it is to red and cooler the closer it is to violet.

The real decision will be made not by consulting the color wheel, but by judging how the flower looks with the rest of the arrangement. Have you ever had trouble determining whether a pair of socks was navy blue or black, depending on what else you compared it to? A red-violet may look warm or cool depending on the other colors in the arrangement.

The best way to master these two exceptions to the rule is to play it by ear—or eye.

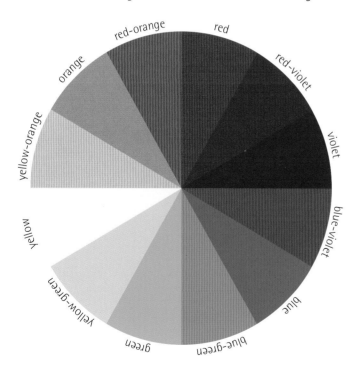

The Color Wheel
Red, yellow and blue are the primary colors. Mix each of these with one of the others to get orange (red and yellow), green (blue and yellow) or violet (red and blue)—the secondary colors. Mix each primary color with the closest secondary color to get everything in between.

Flower Wheel
These colors imitate nature, so flower arranging is the perfect way to use the color wheel.

PASTELS

Pastels generally are just muted versions of the colors on the color wheel. They can be warm or cool.

NEUTRALS

Neutral colors are those that don't seem to make a strong color statement. Light grays, browns and creams fall into this category. In flower arranging you can add most greenery to this category. Green is a prevalent color among flowers, though it's usually overpowered by the flower's blossom. Green stems and foliage in flowers are like blue jeans in clothing: Although green and blue are beautiful colors, they're considered neutral for these purposes.

COMPLEMENTARY COLORS

Even if you want to create a predominantly warm arrangement, sometimes you need a punch of contrast to make things interesting. The contrast can make the impact of the predominant color even more noticeable. To keep an arrangement balanced, again we're going to resort to opposites. A color's opposite is the color directly across it on the color wheel, called its complement. A warm color's complement is cool and vice versa. A little touch of orange in a cool, blue arrangement, for example, emphasizes the blue while adding a little interest to the arrangement.

Exact Complements Go Well Together
This arrangement uses a cool collection of blues from the beads and bowl and green from the foliage. The peach hyacinths add a punch of orange that contrasts and complements the blue without switching the balance away from it.

Close Complements Work, Too
Most of the flowers in this arrangement are a warm yellow-green, the complement of which is red-violet. Although, the container is a cool blue-violet, not the exact complement, it still works. The blue cosmos bring up the violet from the vase and create an appealing color balance.

Chapter One
WARM COLORS

Red, orange and yellow and the colors that appear next to them on the color wheel are warm: crimson, lemon and violet, for example. Warm colors advance, or pop out. They appear closer to you and more intimate. They also are energetic and demand attention. Warm flower arrangements are more likely to be the focal point or a dominant accent in the room.

In nature, warm colors are associated with the sun, bright flowers, fruits and vegetables. Let that liveliness into your home. Use warm arrangements to turn a warm-colored room into a rich and luxurious setting, or let them stand out in a room with a more muted or neutral color scheme. You also can change with the seasons, using warm arrangements to match the season in the summer or to warm up a room in the cooler months.

Daisies in the
WINDOW

These daisies seem to absorb the brightness of the sun and put it on display for you to see. The red provides that punch of color that makes the arrangement exciting, and the peach, coral and yellow soften it to make it just right. Put this arrangement near a window and see if you can keep yourself from smiling as you walk by.

MATERIALS LIST

Silk Flowers
- *36 galax leaves or one bush*
- *3 red gerbera daisy stems*
- *3 yellow gerbera daisy stems*
- *3 peach gerbera daisy stems*
- *3 coral gerbera daisy stems*
- *2 orange Japanese lantern stems*
- *2 yellow Japanese lantern stems*

Other Supplies
- *12½" × 4" × 4" (32cm × 10cm × 10cm) tin container*
- *sheet of Styrofoam*
- *hot glue gun*
- *craft stick*
- *moss*
- *nine 6" (15cm) wooden floral picks*
- *9 ornamental lemon halves*

CUTTING INSTRUCTIONS

* Cut the galax leaves off the stems.

* Cut the daisies to measure about 5" (13cm) from the tip of the stem to the base of the blossom.

* Cut the Japanese lantern stems to varying lengths between 3" (8cm) and 5" (13cm).

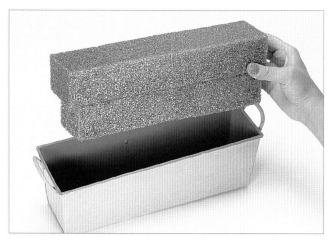

1 CUT FOAM

Cut two blocks of Styrofoam each to 11" × 3" (28cm × 8cm). Taper one on all four sides until it will sit in the bottom of the container. Use a craft stick to run hot glue along the outside edges of the blocks, and adhere them together with the tapered side on the bottom. Don't apply glue over the top of either block because the flowers won't go through glue easily.

Drizzle hot glue along the bottom of the container, and let it set for a second. Drop the Styrofoam into the container with the smaller block on the bottom. Tin doesn't always lie flat, so press down to make sure the Styrofoam adheres to the entire surface.

2 COVER WITH MOSS

Use a craft stick to run hot glue around the top edges of the Styrofoam and along the top inner edges of the container. Cover the block with moss, tucking the moss between the block and container. Press down to make sure it adheres.

3 COVER CONTAINER WITH LEAVES

Hot glue the galax leaves over the entire container. Cover the bottom first, then cover the top edge, gluing each leaf so it points upward and overlaps the moss a bit. Then cover the middle area, arranging the leaves so they all point downward. Fold the tips of the leaves around the bottom edge and glue them down. Work on the corners last. Glue down any part of a leaf sticking up, and then glue down another leaf, folding it around the corner.

4 INSERT RED DAISIES

Red is the dominant color in this arrangement, so add the red daisies first. Then you can arrange the other colors around them. Insert one daisy in each front corner. Add the other in the middle toward the back.

5) INSERT YELLOW, PEACH AND CORAL DAISIES

After red, yellow is the next dominant color. Add the yellow daisies, staggering them as you did the red daisies and pushing them in at different angles and to different depths. Insert one peach daisy on one side and one coral daisy on the other side, both centered between front and back. These daisies are close enough in color to balance each other but different enough to provide a little variety. Insert the four remaining daisies at different angles and depths to fill in as needed.

6) INSERT LEMONS

Insert the sharp end of a floral pick into the back of each lemon. Insert them randomly to fill in the arrangement. Vary the depths a bit to make it interesting, but don't let them stick out so much as to change the shape of the arrangement. As you insert the lemons, try to apply pressure on the pick instead of the lemon itself or you'll push the pick through the entire lemon.

7) INSERT JAPANESE LANTERNS

If any blossoms fell off while you were cutting the stems, hot glue them back on. Randomly insert the lanterns and any leftover foliage throughout the arrangement. Step back frequently to make sure you're keeping it balanced. These small, light flowers contrast the larger daisy blossoms and make the arrangement more fun. Let some lanterns hang over the edge of the container, and let some leaves stick out among the daisies to add more dimension.

GIVE IT A DIFFERENT LOOK

Make this arrangement bright and sunny by using all yellow gerbera daisies for a monochromatic look.

Field of Wild-
FLOWERS

These vibrant yellows aren't normally mixed in nature because the flowers come from different seasons. But that's the nice thing about working with silk flowers. You can use any flowers you like to create the arrangement perfect for your needs. In this case, I wanted a strong, bright yellow arrangement, and these are the flowers that do the job.

MATERIALS LIST

Silk Flowers
- 4 yellow black-eyed Susan stems
- 4 yellow sunflower stems
- 5 yellow oncidium orchid stems
- 4 yellow astilbe stems
- 1 long grass bush
- 1 grape ivy bush
- 1 corkscrew willow stem with foliage, about 5' (153cm) tall

Other Supplies
- 9½" × 5" × 5½" (24cm × 13cm × 13cm) neutral-colored, glazed container
- yellow or saffron spray paint
- copper spray paint
- 2 blocks of dry floral foam
- hot glue gun
- moss
- scissors
- heavy-duty wire cutters
- pliers
- 24-gauge floral wire

CUTTING INSTRUCTIONS

✳ Cut all the flowers to approximately 16" (41cm).

✳ Cut the grass bush into individual blades.

✳ Cut sprigs of about 6" (15cm) from the ivy bush.

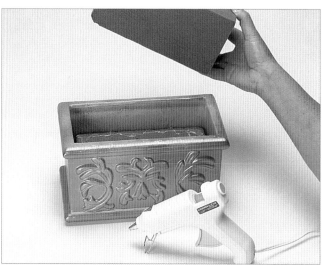

1) PAINT CONTAINER

Spray paint the container with two even coats of yellow or saffron, letting it dry after each coat. Spray paint a layer of copper over the container, letting some of the yellow show through.

2) ADD FOAM BLOCKS

Apply hot glue all over the inside bottom of the container. Insert one foam block and push down so it adheres to the bottom of the container. Run hot glue around the top outside edges of this block of foam, and place the second block on top. Again apply pressure to make sure it adheres.

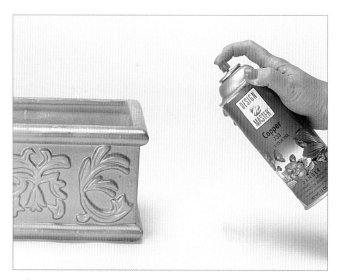

3) ADD MOSS

Lay a sheet of moss over the container and foam blocks, and trim it to the size of the container with scissors. Apply hot glue around the outside edges of the foam block and adhere the moss. Once the glue dries, you can spray the moss with water to keep it from becoming too dusty.

4) INSERT BLACK-EYED SUSANS

Each type of flower in this arrangement will form a different row. Insert the black-eyed Susan stems on the left side, one in front of the other.

5) INSERT SUNFLOWERS

Insert the sunflower stems slightly to the left of center, again placing one in front of the other. I decided to place the sunflowers here instead of on the end because they naturally face straight up.

6) INSERT ORCHIDS

Insert the orchids slightly right of center, one in front of the other. If you have any shorter sprigs left over from cutting the orchid stems, you can insert them in this row to help fill it out.

7) INSERT ASTILBES

Add a row of astilbes on the right side. Insert each stem so the lower sprigs face outward and hang over the edge a bit.

Design Tips

* Even though you're forming rows, they don't have to be perfect. It's more interesting to create some variety in how the flowers lie.

* As you insert the flowers, spread the blossoms out.

* Push the front and back flowers in each row a bit deeper than the rest to give the arrangement some nice shape.

* Bend the stems of any flower that sits along the outside edge of the arrangement so the flower faces out a bit. This makes the arrangement interesting from all angles.

8) BRING ROWS TOGETHER WITH GRASS

Insert one stem of grass in each corner of the container and one in the center of the arrangement. Blend the grass among the blossoms with your fingers.

9) FILL IN WITH IVY

Insert some ivy sprigs around the perimeter of the container so they hang down over the edge. Insert shorter sprigs deeper in the arrangement to fill in as needed. Save just a few for later.

10) TIE IT TOGETHER WITH WILLOW

Cut the willow just below the foliage with heavy-duty wire cutters. Use a pair of pliers to clean up and smooth any sharp edges or wires. Bend the willow a bit so it will be easier to wrap around the arrangement. Wrap the willow around all of the stems, just above the ivy, so the two ends of the willow meet in the back. Bind the ends together with a 9" (23cm) length of wire. Trim the ends of the wire and tuck them into the arrangement. Allow a few pieces of willow to hang out loosely, but if any stick out more than you'd like, hold them in place with wire.

11) COVER WIRE

Use spare ivy sprigs to cover any visible wire. If necessary, you can hot glue a leaf directly over the wire.

GIVE IT A DIFFERENT LOOK

Want to change this to a fall arrangement? Get inspired by rich fall colors such as rust, plum and orange. Leave in the sunflowers, then add mums, purple daisies, statice, cattails and wheat.

Roses by Candle-LIGHT

These warm, rich purples and reds set the mood for a quiet night. Surrounded by cooler-colored flowers, the purple itself would seem cool. But the luxurious reds and the reassuring candlelight make this arrangement perfect for an intimate gathering.

MATERIALS LIST

Silk Flowers
6 red anemone stems
3 purple ranunculus sprays, 2
* blossoms and a bud on each*
24 lavender stems or 1 bush
2 button fern stems
2 red berry stems

Other Supplies
8" × 5" (20cm × 13cm) plum or
* purple ceramic vase*
sheet of Styrofoam
hot glue gun
craft sticks
floral adhesive
4 plastic candleholders
two 7" (18cm) plum candles
two 7" (18cm) red candles

CUTTING INSTRUCTIONS

* Cut each anemone so the stem measures 2" (5cm) from the tip of the stem to the base of the blossom.

* Cut each ranunculus to measure 3" (8cm) from the tip of the stem to the base of the blossom.

* Cut each lavender stem to measure 1" (3cm) from the tip of the stem to the base of the blossom.

* Cut sprigs of button fern with 1" (3cm) stems.

* Cut sprigs of berries at varying lengths but no longer than 1" (3cm) stems.

1) CUT FOAM TO FIT VASE

Cut a piece of Styrofoam to 4" × 7" (10cm × 18cm). Cut another to 5½" × 3" (14cm × 8cm). Imprint the shape of the opening into the smaller block to determine the exact size you need. Then taper both blocks as needed to fit. They should fit snugly to provide stability for the candleholders. Run hot glue around the edges of the blocks with a craft stick, and glue them together. Drizzle hot glue over the bottom of the container, then press the foam into the vase.

2) INSERT CANDLEHOLDERS

Apply floral adhesive liberally to the bottoms of the candleholders. Insert them in an even row into the center of the Styrofoam. If they don't look perfectly straight, lightly tap on them with a hammer to straighten them. Floral adhesive stabilizes the candleholders so that you can change candles easily.

3) INSERT ANEMONES

Put floral adhesive on the tip of each stem before inserting it. Put one red anemone on the left side and one on the right. Add two more on the back and two on the front. Remember that you don't want the arrangement to be perfectly symmetrical.

4) INSERT RANUNCULUSES

Insert the candles in the holders. Add a ring of paper in the holder to make the candles fit tighter if necessary. Insert two of the larger ranunculuses in the front, one sitting high and one low. Do the same in the back. Insert two smaller ranunculus blossoms on the left side and two on the right side. Randomly insert the buds to fill holes.

5) INSERT LAVENDER STEMS

Randomly insert the lavender sprigs, some up high, some lower, all angled differently. Push the stems deep into the foam. The lavender stems should extend farther from the arrangement than the other flowers. This adds contrast and extra dimension.

6) INSERT BUTTON FERN

Randomly insert the button fern sprigs. Let longer ones hang down over the edge of the container. Try to maintain a balanced look as you insert them.

7) INSERT BERRIES

Randomly insert the berry sprigs. Use any extra berries or button fern you need to fill in holes or achieve a good balance.

GIVE IT A DIFFERENT LOOK

Use taper candles at varying heights for a more dramatic arrangement. Or add some color contrast by taking out the red anemones and using orange ranunculus and bittersweet instead.

Fruit and Flower
BOWL

This arrangement borrows from all the warm colors. The flowers are red-orange and yellow-orange, and the apples themselves have a bit of red and a bit of yellow in them. This bright and fun arrangement can go anywhere from the kitchen or dining room to the living room or patio.

I used a bowl with red swirls painted onto the glass. You can imitate this effect with red three-dimensional paint, found in the fabric painting section of your local craft store. If you want thin lines, dry the paint immediately with a hair dryer before it begins to settle and thicken. Either way, let the paint dry completely overnight before you start arranging.

MATERIALS LIST

Silk Flowers
15 green boxwood stems
9 red-orange cosmos sprays
24 gold pom-pom mum stems

Other Supplies
8" (20cm) clear glass bowl
twenty 2" (5cm) red apples
8" (20cm) Styrofoam ball
hot glue gun
moss
scissors

CUTTING INSTRUCTIONS

* Push the leaves on the boxwood stems as far as they will go toward the blossoms. This makes the sprigs denser so they will provide better coverage. Cut sprigs that measure 1" (3cm) from the tips of the stems to the bottoms of the sprays.

* Cut each cosmos to measure 5" (13cm) from the tip of the stem to the base of the blossom. Trim off any foliage or nodules so the stem will go into the Styrofoam easily.

* Cut the pom-pom mums to about 7" (18cm). Remove all foliage except from the very top.

1) INSERT FOAM BALL

Fill the bowl with apples. Cut the bottom of the Styrofoam ball so it sits snugly in the bowl's opening over the apples. Apply hot glue around the outside edge of the ball, then slide it into the bowl. Clean up any glue that dripped down too far from the rim so flowers and foliage don't stick to it later.

2) COVER WITH MOSS

Apply hot glue in spots on the back of the moss. Remember that hot glue will keep stems from going into the ball, so use only as much as you need. Flip the moss over and place it over the ball. Trim extra moss with scissors.

Design Tip

When working with a circular arrangement or any centerpiece arrangement, try placing your arrangement on a lazy Susan so you can rotate it with ease. This also helps you create a balanced arrangement.

3) INSERT BOXWOOD

Start inserting the sprigs at the top of the ball and work your way down in rings or spirals until you've covered the entire ball.

4) INSERT COSMOS

Insert the cosmos so they're facing straight out, parallel to the surface of the ball. Insert one flower in the top of the ball. A bit farther down, insert a loose ring of cosmos, and so on until you've created a ring above the bowl. Leave room to alternate pom-poms with the cosmos. Randomly insert the remaining cosmos buds.

5) INSERT POM POMS

Insert the pom-poms as you did the cosmos, starting at the top and alternating with the cosmos. Turn the bowl as you work to keep the flowers balanced.

GIVE IT A DIFFERENT LOOK

Change the fruit in the bowl to kiwis, blueberries, raspberries or mix up different small fruits. Then add touches of coordinating color in the arrangement with filler flowers.

Drama in the
JUNGLE

Perfect for a romantic bedroom or as the dramatic focal point in any room with a rich color scheme, this arrangement is designed to stand out. It's dense, full and layered like the jungle. From any side or from the top, the flowers and foliage sit at different heights and depths. There's so much to look at, you'll never tire of this arrangement, no matter where you put it.

MATERIALS LIST

Silk Flowers
3 bamboo leaf foliage stems
3 red ginger stems
3 red tropical heliconia stems
3 yellow-orange calla lily stems
3 green calla lily stems
3 red-green anthurium stems
3 red anthurium stems
3 Japanese maple foliage sprays
3 large bamboo palm foliage stems
1 horsetail branch or several horsetail stalks

Other Supplies
8" × 9½" (20cm × 24cm) Oriental basket
3 blocks of dry floral foam
hot glue gun
moss

CUTTING INSTRUCTIONS

* Cut the bamboo leaf foliage stems (you also can use small bamboo palm foliage) to about 22" (56cm).

* Cut the red ginger stems to varying lengths between 17" (43cm) and 22" (56cm). Smooth and curl the leaves for a more natural look.

* Cut the heliconia stems to 18" (46cm).

* Cut one yellow-orange calla lily to 11" (28cm) and the other two to 9" (23cm).

* Cut the green calla lilies to 14" (36cm).

* Cut the red-green anthuriums to about 11" (28cm).

* Cut one red anthurium to 17" (43cm) and the other two to 11" (28cm).

* Cut the Japanese maple foliage sprays to 26" (66cm).

* Cut the large bamboo palm foliage to about 15" (38cm).

* Cut the horsetail branch or stalks to 28" (71cm).

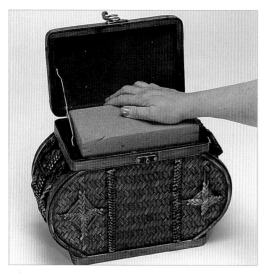

1) INSERT FOAM

Glue the foam blocks into a stack with a layer of hot glue along the outer edges between the blocks. Put hot glue over the bottom of the basket and drop the stack in. Push down to make sure the foam adheres to the basket.

2) COVER WITH MOSS

Some of the foam should be sticking above the sides of the basket. Apply hot glue to these sides, not the top, of the foam. Cover the foam with moss and tuck the moss between the foam and the basket, making sure it sticks to the glue.

3) INSERT BAMBOO LEAF FOLIAGE

Insert the bamboo leaf foliage stems in a group just left of center, all leaning back slightly. Vary the height of each for some variety.

4) INSERT GINGER

Insert the tallest ginger stem in the middle of the bamboo leaf foliage. Insert another stem to the left of the group and push it into the foam a bit farther. Insert the last one to the right of the group, and push it down the farthest. Insert the two shorter ginger stems at slight angles to add interest.

5) INSERT HELICONIA

Insert one heliconia stem in the back center of the group of stems you've already inserted. Let it sit fairly high and straight. Insert another in the front of the group, slightly to the left of center. Push it down farther and insert it at an angle so it leans forward a bit. Insert the last one into the center of the group at an extreme angle so it hangs over the opposite side of the basket.

6) INSERT YELLOW-ORANGE CALLA LILIES

Insert one of the short lilies into the side of the foam in the center of the basket so it lies horizontally. Insert the other two in the center of the basket, a bit to the right of the other group of stems. Push the lilies in so they sit fairly low. Bend one stem so the lily hangs in front of the basket and slightly to the right.

7) INSERT GREEN CALLA LILIES

Insert one green lily in the back right corner and bend the stem so it leans outward. Insert another in the back closer to the middle and bend the stem so it leans toward the front right corner. Insert the last one in the back left corner behind the heliconia. Bend it down quite a bit so it hangs down over the edge of the basket. Also bend it forward.

8) INSERT RED-GREEN ANTHURIUM

Insert one red-green anthurium in the front left corner and bend it down over the corner to balance the
green calla lily in the back right corner. Bend the
stem down, but bend the flower itself back up to
show it off. Insert another red-green anthurium in
the back left corner and bend it outward. Insert the
third anthurium in the middle of the left side, just
barely leaning forward. Push it farther into the foam
so it doesn't sit quite so high.

9) INSERT RED ANTHURIUM

Insert the tallest red anthurium in the center of the
ginger blossoms. Insert a shorter red anthurium in
the front right center of this main group. Insert the
last red anthurium in the front left corner of the
basket. The two shorter anthuriums should sit low
and lean forward.

10) INSERT JAPANESE MAPLE FOLIAGE

Insert one spray of foliage just slightly to the left of
center of the main grouping, just behind the tallest
red anthurium. Insert another at the front of this
group and push it all the way into the foam. Insert
the last spray to the right of center of this group
and push it all the way down. Spread the foliage
out, both side to side and backward and forward so
the sprays don't look like fans.

12) INSERT HORSETAIL

Fan out the sprigs, and insert the stem just slightly to the left of the center of the basket, sitting straight up. Spread the sprigs out among the rest of the foliage and flowers.

11) INSERT LARGE BAMBOO PALM FOLIAGE

Insert one palm foliage stem to the right of the center of the basket, pushing it as deep as possible. Bend the stem and open up the foliage in a way that faces outward. Put another in the back left corner of the basket, again pushing it as deep as possible, and spread out the leaves. Insert the last stem in the center of the basket at an angle so it leans forward and to the right.

GIVE IT A DIFFERENT LOOK

To give this arrangement a softer look, substitute the heliconia with dendrobium or oncidium orchids.

Chapter Two
COOL COLORS

Blue, green and purple and the colors next to them
on the color wheel are cool. Cool colors are perfect for creating
calm and serene schemes throughout your décor. Unlike warm colors,
which stand out, cool colors recede. They step back and allow you to
absorb their beauty. In a flower arrangement, they add a sense of con-
tentment and comfort, peace and quiet with their presence, without
overloading your senses.

Cool colors, such as aquas, lavenders and greens, bring forth images
of the more magnificent aspects of nature. A broad expanse of sky, a
deep ocean, a still lake or a stretching green meadow. And just as the
warm sun punctuates the sky or bright wildflowers accent a meadow,
you can add small spots of warm color to these arrangements to bring
them together.

Springtime
BREEZE

These silver pussy willows bring the white and blue flowers together and give the arrangement a woodsy, natural feel despite the lack of "natural" greens and browns. Put it in a neutral room to add that extra touch or in a patio or sunroom to bridge the worlds of indoors and out.

MATERIALS LIST

Silk Flowers

3 pussy willow branches with wooden stems
1 dogwood blossom stem
3 blue hyacinth stems with 2 blossoms each
1 blue hydrangea bush with 3 large blossoms and 1 small blossom

Other Supplies

7½" (19cm) clear cylindrical vase
hot glue gun
craft stick
3½lbs (1½kg) décor sand

CUTTING INSTRUCTIONS

✳ Cut the pussy willow branches to different lengths between 14" (36cm) and 20" (51cm). Handle the pussy willow gently to keep the willow from falling off.

✳ Cut the dogwood stem to 18" (46cm).

✳ Cut the blue hyacinths to 16" (41cm).

✳ Cut four 10" (25cm) sprigs from the hydrangea bush.

1 GLUE PUSSY WILLOWS TO VASE

Spread out the pussy willow stems on each branch a bit. Run hot glue along the bottom half of the back of each branch and glue them around the exterior of the vase. Leave some space between the branches so you can see through. Fill in empty areas with smaller branches or individual stems. Peel off excess glue when it has started to cool. Pour half of the sand into the vase.

2 INSERT DOGWOOD

Insert the dogwood stem in the middle of the vase and push it all the way to the bottom.

3 INSERT HYACINTHS

Bend and curl the leaves of the hyacinths to add interest. Insert the stems in a triangular arrangement around the center. Spread the flowers and foliage out. You can even bend some so they hang out of the arrangement over the edge of the vase.

4) INSERT HYDRANGEA

Add the rest of the sand to the vase. Remove any foliage near the bottom of the hydrangea sprigs so they'll enter the sand easily. Insert the smallest sprig in the center of the arrangement and the other three in a triangular arrangement around the outside.

GIVE IT A DIFFERENT LOOK

Change this to a wintery white arrangement by using paperwhites and winterberry and covering the container with birch branches.

Tropical
OASIS

You might expect to see this arrangement near the pool at a resort or in a desert-like setting. The bowl and marbles leave you no choice but to think of a refreshing splash of water. The small specks of peach-pink hyacinths just make the cool greens and blues seem stronger in contrast. Use this arrangement as a spot of cool in an otherwise warm room to really make it stand out.

MATERIALS LIST

Silk Flowers
1 tropical palm bush
3 peach-pink hyacinth stems, at least 2 blossoms per stem
2 green-yellow berry branches

Other Supplies
9" (23cm) turquoise mosaic bowl
4" (10cm) Styrofoam disk
hot glue gun
6 bags of soft blue and turquoise marbles or pebbles

CUTTING INSTRUCTIONS

❄ Cut four 14" (36cm) sprigs off the berry branches.

1) INSERT TROPICAL PALM

Glue the Styrofoam disk in the center of the bowl with hot glue. Spread out the branches of the palm bush and insert it into the middle of the disk.

2) INSERT HYACINTHS

Gently curve the foliage of the hyacinths to give it shape. Insert the hyacinths near the center of the foam disk in a triangular arrangement around the palm bush. Push the hyacinths all the way into the foam.

3) INSERT BERRIES

Spread out the leaves and berries on the berry sprigs. Insert each sprig on a different side of the grouping.

4) SHAPE BERRIES

Bend the berry stems so they stick out a bit from the arrangement to add a little interest and dimension.

5) ADD MARBLES OR PEBBLES

Pour the marbles into the bowl. If you have several different varieties of size and color, mix them in another bowl first.

GIVE IT A DIFFERENT LOOK

Fill out this arrangement even more by substituting the hyacinths with large orchids or spray orchids and adding lily grass.

Cool Candle
WREATH

The flowers and blue glass of this centerpiece are a calming, cool color. The warm-colored lemons contrast nicely and will bring out the warm feeling of the candle's flame. For a completely cool arrangement, fill the vase with cool-colored glass beads or let the candle stand alone. Try putting this arrangement on the mantelpiece or on a side table as a pleasing accent to the rest of your décor.

MATERIALS LIST

Silk Flowers
1 ivy twig wreath, 10" (25cm) or 12" (30cm) wide
1 viburnum stem
4 blue iris stems
1 blue statice bush
1 green button flower stem or any small green flower

Other Supplies
20" × 6" (51cm × 15cm) tall translucent blue vase, optional
9" × 3" (23cm × 8cm) yellow, blue, white or multi-colored pillar candle, optional
thirty-six 1½" (40mm) ornamental lemons, optional
hot glue gun
craft sticks

CUTTING INSTRUCTIONS

※ Trim 2" to 3" (5cm to 8cm) sprigs from the viburnum stem.

※ Cut the irises to measure 2" (5cm) from the tip of the stem to the base of the flower.

※ Cut the blue statice blossoms off the bush fairly close to the bases of the blossoms to varying lengths between 5" (13cm) and 8" (20cm) from the tip of the stem to the top of the flower.

※ Cut sprigs of green button flower to measure about 3" (8cm).

1) FILL VASE WITH LEMONS

Insert the candle into the vase. Pour the lemons around it. This arrangement is cool, but the warm yellow lemons add a pleasant contrast. For an extremely cool arrangement, try adding cool blue marbles or nothing at all.

2) ADD VIBURNUM

Place the wreath around the base of the candle. Use a craft stick to apply hot glue to the tips of the viburnum stems, and insert them into the wreath every few inches. Don't worry about making the arrangement balanced at this point.

3) ADD IRISES

Glue the four irises into the wreath randomly with hot glue and a craft stick.

4) ADD BLUE STATICE STEMS

Apply hot glue to the tips of the blue statice stems with a craft stick and insert them into the wreath. Hold them in place with a craft stick until the glue dries. Insert the stems at different angles and depths for variety. Let some hang over the wreath for a loose, natural garden look.

5) ADD BUTTON FLOWER

Insert the button flower sprigs in all different directions, gluing them to the wreath with hot glue and a craft stick. Fill in any holes in the wreath with extra foliage from the various flowers. Remove any loose strings of hot glue.

GIVE IT A DIFFERENT LOOK

For a quick new look, change the color of the hurricane and the candle. Or go green by substituting the lemons with limes, and using a clear hurricane, a lime green candle, and white tulips in place of the irises.

Soft Flowers and
FABRIC

These yellow-green orchids could be considered either warm or cool. With flowers like this, use the container to tip the scales in the direction you need. I used a cooler, sea foam green fabric to accentuate the green in the flowers, swinging the arrangement over to the cool side. The lavender blossoms and the ribbon also bring out the cool purple at the center of the orchids. Put these flowers in the bathroom or any casual room that needs a little brightening up.

MATERIALS LIST

Silk Flowers
- 1 lavender bush
- 3 sea green-lavender phalaenopsis orchid stems

Other Supplies
- 4" (10cm) terra cotta pot
- masking or electrical tape
- sand
- sheet of Styrofoam
- hot glue gun
- circular piece of sea-green sheer fabric with wired edge, 26" (66cm) in diameter
- 2 bags of pearlized iridescent crystal fiber (Easter grass)
- 4 greening pins
- 1 thick rubber band
- lavender wired ribbon, 3" (8cm) wide

CUTTING INSTRUCTIONS

- Cut the orchid stems to 20" (51cm).
- Cut a length of ribbon about 48" (122cm).

1) INSERT FOAM

Cover the hole at the bottom of the pot with tape. Pour about 2" (5cm) of sand into the pot to give it weight and stability. Press the Styrofoam sheet onto the top of the pot to make an imprint and cut along the inside of the line. Apply hot glue around the edges of the Styrofoam and insert it into the pot. It should sit above the edges of the pot just a little.

2) INSERT LAVENDER BUSH

Insert the lavender bush in the center of the Styrofoam and spread the stems out.

3) INSERT ORCHIDS

Insert the orchid stems in a triangular arrangement around the lavender bush. Mix the orchid petals and lavender blossoms together so they look natural.

4) GATHER FABRIC AROUND POT

Lay the circular fabric flat. Place the pot in the center. Attach the crystal fiber to the Styrofoam with greening pins, letting it hang down around the pot. Lay some additional fibers on the fabric around the pot as well. The fabric itself is sheer, so these fibers will hide the pot and add some volume to the fabric. Gather the fabric around the pot and secure it with a rubber band around the stems. Pull some of the fabric back out to fluff and shape it.

5) TIE BOW

Wrap the ribbon around the rubber band and tie a large bow. Shape the bow loops, and trim and scallop the ends of the ribbon.

GIVE IT A DIFFERENT LOOK

For a fuller arrangement that's quick and easy, simply put an ivy bush in the vase and insert a pink geranium bush inside it.

Chapter Three
PASTELS

Pastels are muted versions of warm and cool colors.
They're softer and understated, so while they create less impact, they
add that soft touch, that little something, that brings the room together.
They can be fragile, soft and lively all at once. Like cool colors, pastels are
calm and serene, demanding less attention. And like warm colors, they can
add a bit more energy, a bit of joy or whimsy.

Pastels nurture, giving you the safe, snug, loved feeling of warm colors
and the calm reassurance of cool colors. When nature wants to give you
the best of both worlds, it uses pastels, such as powder blue, rose, pink,
lime green and soft yellow.

Baby's Breath
TOPIARY

The surprise of this arrangement helps it stand out despite its quiet colors. Baby's breath normally acts as a filler in flower arrangements. Making it the focus of an entire arrangement lends a bit of drama and irony to the muted pastel colors that surround it. Add this arrangement to any room that needs a touch of fun or light-hearted joy.

MATERIALS LIST

Silk Flowers
   5 baby's breath stems
   1 small grape ivy bush

Other Supplies
   5" × 6" (13cm × 15cm) white
     ceramic container
   lavender spray paint
   sheet of Styrofoam
   hot glue gun
   foam glue
   moss
   double-sided purple-blue wired
     ribbon, ½" (15mm) wide

CUTTING INSTRUCTIONS

✳ Cut three stems of baby's breath to 21" (53cm) and two stems to 19" (48cm).

✳ Trim sprigs from the ivy bush to varying lengths between 5" (13cm) and 7" (18cm). Trim any foliage and nodules near the bottom to make sure the sprigs enter the foam easily.

✳ Cut a 48" (122cm) length of ribbon.

1 PAINT CONTAINER AND CUT FOAM

Spray paint the container. Set it aside to dry. Cut two pieces of Styrofoam, each measuring 3½" × 3½" (9cm × 9cm). Glue the Styrofoam blocks together by running hot glue around the outside edges where the blocks meet. Hold until they feel secure. My container is 6" (15cm) wide at its widest point, but the opening is only 4" (10cm) wide. If your container is different, just make sure you cut the Styrofoam to dimensions slightly smaller than the opening.

2 GLUE FOAM INTO CONTAINER

Apply foam glue to the bottom of the container and to the bottom of the Styrofoam. Secure the foam to the bottom of the container.

3 COVER WITH MOSS

Apply hot glue to the top of the Styrofoam at each corner. Let the glue set for about 10 seconds. Place a small sheet of moss over the Styrofoam and tuck it into the container. The moss doesn't have to adhere perfectly. The flower stems you're inserting later will help hold it in place.

4 INSERT BABY'S BREATH

Gather the five stems of baby's breath with the tallest ones in the center. Insert the cluster into the center of the Styrofoam. If they didn't go in straight, simply bend the stems near the bottoms. Spread the baby's breath by bending the stems outward to create a fuller appearance.

5) INSERT IVY

Insert the longest sprigs around the edges of the container, bending the stems downward so the leaves will hang over the edge of the container. Insert the shorter sprigs closer to the center of the arrangement to cover the moss.

6) TIE BOW

Tie a shoestring bow tightly around the base of the baby's breath to form the topiary shape. Tie a double knot to secure it. Trim the ends of the ribbon to your desired length. Fold the end of the ribbon in half and cut in a diagonal to form a v-shaped end.

GIVE IT A DIFFERENT LOOK

For a burst of color, substitute the baby's breath with alstroemeria or gerbera daisies. Paint the container to match the flower color.

Blue Cosmos Center-
PIECE

The yellow-green hydrangeas and lime green dahlias in this arrangement could be considered warm, but the warm flowers simply help the blue cosmos, the dominant color in the arrangement, stand out and seem even cooler in contrast. The blue vase and green foliage also lend a cooler feeling. This arrangement will take on the casual mood or the touch of elegance of whatever décor you pair it with.

MATERIALS LIST

Silk Flowers

3 yellow-green hydrangea stems

3 lime green dahlia stems, 2 blossoms per stem (mums or zinnias also will work)

4 blue cosmos stems, 2 blossoms and a bud per stem (add more for more color)

1 small frosted ivy bush

Other Supplies

10¼" × 5¼" (26cm × 13cm) blue ceramic vase

sand

foam glue

craft stick

6" (15cm) Styrofoam ball

hot glue gun

24-gauge gold wire

two 3" (8cm) wired wooden floral picks

CUTTING INSTRUCTIONS

✳ Cut the hydrangeas to measure 3" (8cm) from the tip of the stem to the base of the flower. Trim off any leaves below the blossoms so the stem will enter the ball easily.

✳ Cut the dahlia blossoms to measure 3" (8cm) from the tip of the stem to the base of the blossom. Remove most of the foliage. Trim the extra leaves to have a 1" (3cm) stem.

✳ Cut sprigs of blue cosmos to varying lengths between 3" (8cm) and 4" (10cm).

✳ Cut sprigs from the ivy bush varying in length from 4" (10cm) to 9" (23cm). Make sure each sprig has 1" (3cm) of clean stem so it will enter the ball easily.

✳ Cut a 9' (3m) length of wire.

1 WEIGH DOWN VASE
Fill the vase with sand to weigh it down.

Technique Tip

To make large blossoms with short stems stick more securely into the foam, start a hole with the stem, remove it, add a bit of foam glue to the hole, and reinsert the stem.

2 GLUE IN FOAM BALL
Apply foam glue sparingly around the inside of the rim of the vase with a craft stick. Place the Styrofoam ball into the opening and apply pressure until the glue sets.

3 INSERT HYDRANGEAS
Bend each stem just below the blossom. Insert the stems in a triangular arrangement around the top of the ball so they hang down.

4 INSERT DAHLIAS AROUND TOP
Randomly insert half of the dahlia blossoms to tightly fill the top half of the arrangement. Leave about 1" (3cm) of the stem exposed.

5) INSERT DAHLIAS AROUND BOTTOM

Randomly insert the rest of the dahlias around the hydrangea blossoms to fill in the lower half of the Styrofoam ball.

6) INSERT BLUE COSMOS ON TOP

Insert the two cosmos sprigs with the longest stems in the top of the ball to fill in the hole.

7) FILL IN WITH REST OF COSMOS

Insert two more cosmos sprigs between each hydrangea cluster. Stagger the heights of the cosmos. Feel free to add more than four stems of blue cosmos for more color.

8) PLACE IVY AROUND BOTTOM

Insert three of the longest ivy sprigs around the base of the arrangement. Then shape them to hang down over the vase.

9 FILL IN WITH REST OF IVY

Bend the stems of the rest of the ivy sprigs downward, randomly inserting them throughout the arrangement to fill any holes. Insert the stems higher than where you want the foliage to lie. Then mold the ivy around the ball to cover any exposed foam and make the arrangement appear tight.

10 ADD DAHLIA FOLIAGE

Fill in any remaining gaps with the extra dahlia foliage. Shape and mold the leaves to look natural.

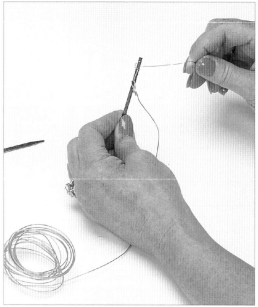

11 GLUE IN HYDRANGEA TIPS

To round out the shape of the arrangement, hot glue the tips of the hydrangeas to the rim of the vase. Hold each blossom in place with a craft stick until the glue dries.

12 ATTACH WIRE TO FLORAL PICK

Wrap the gold wire around the floral pick, combining it with the pick wire as you wrap.

13 WRAP WIRE

Insert the pick into the top of the arrangement as deep as it will go. Wrap the wire somewhat tightly around the arrangement. Intertwine the wire with the blossoms and foliage as you would the lights on a holiday tree. To secure the wire in place at various points, wrap it around the stem of a leaf.

14 SECURE WIRE

Wrap the other end of the gold wire around another wired wooden pick and insert the pick into the bottom of the arrangement.

GIVE IT A DIFFERENT LOOK

For a monochromatic arrangement, change all the flowers to shades of green. Or soften the arrangement by using pink hydrangea instead of blue cosmos.

Playful
DAISIES

Everyone needs a bit of humor in their lives. With a spirit of fun, the yellows in this arrangement convey humor and playfulness. To emphasize a different color, simply use different markers or make another color more dominant. Notice, though, that the white background of the pot really lets the yellow daisies shine. Perfect for a playroom, nursery or any place in which you want to lighten the mood.

MATERIALS LIST

Silk Flowers
2 river oat stems with foliage (wired grass or dracaena leaves also will work)
3 yellow wild daisy sprays with green centers (regular daisies also will work)
3 yellow acacia stems

Other Supplies
4" (10cm) clay pot
foam brush
white acrylic paint
lime green Flexi Foam
ruler
scissors
hot glue gun
lime green-turquoise fringe
craft stick
light blue, light green and yellow terra cotta markers
clear glaze gloss finish protective spray
1 block dry floral foam
moss

CUTTING INSTRUCTIONS

* Cut 18" (46cm) of fringe.

* Cut two sprigs of river oats to 17" (43cm). Cut the remaining sprigs so they have 3" (8cm) stems. You'll also have some sprigs with foliage but no oats left over.

* Cut two daisy sprays to about 16" (41cm). Cut the remaining daisies into sprigs about 11" (28cm) long.

* Cut three 15" (38cm) acacia sprigs and six 8" (20cm) to 10" (25cm) sprigs.

PAINT POT

Using the foam brush, paint the pot white. You do not have to paint the rim.

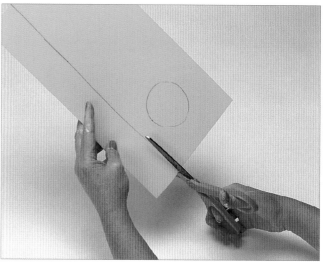

MAKE RIM FOR POT

Cut a 16" × 2" (41cm × 5cm) strip of Flexi Foam. Also cut a circle with a 3½" (9cm) diameter.

TRIM FOAM STRIP

Glue the circle to the bottom of the pot with a hot glue gun. Wrap the strip of foam you cut in step 2 around the rim of the pot. Secure one end with hot glue. Trim the other end so the two ends will meet perfectly when both are glued down.

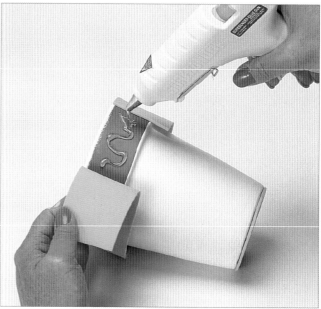

GLUE DOWN FOAM STRIP

Glue the foam down all the way around the rim. Hold the foam in place until the glue dries. The foam stretches a bit, so you can stretch the ends to make them meet, if necessary. Glue the very end down smoothly so the seam is barely visible.

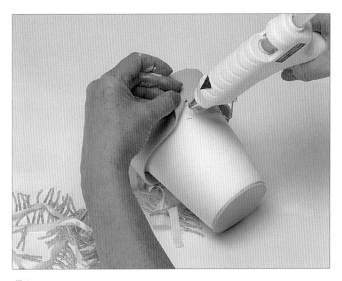

5) ATTACH FRINGE

Glue one end of the fringe at a spot just below the rim of the pot. The foam strip you glued around the rim of the pot will cover the very top of the fringe. Wrap the fringe around the pot and glue it down as you go. You can use a craft stick to hold it in place in each spot as it dries.

6) DECORATE POT

Decorate the pot with the yellow, green and blue markers. These markers pick up colors from the flowers, foam and fringe. To make the design last longer, spray the pot with a protective spray.

7) INSERT FOAM BLOCK

Cut the foam block to 4" (10cm) tall. Trim it to measure 3½" (9cm) at the top, tapering to 2" (5cm) at the bottom. It doesn't have to look perfect; it just has to fit snugly down to the bottom of the pot. Apply hot glue over all the sides of the foam block, especially the corner edges. Don't apply glue to the top. Push it into the pot and move on to the next step before the glue dries.

8 COVER WITH MOSS

Lay moss over the foam block and tuck it between the pot and the foam block. Press the moss to the hot glue you applied in the last step.

9 INSERT RIVER OATS

Insert the two tallest river oat sprigs in the center of the foam. Spread the oats and stems any way you like. Then insert the shorter sprigs around the base of the arrangement.

10 INSERT RIVER OATS FOLIAGE

Curl the foliage on the leftover river oat sprigs with your hands. These spirals will provide the whimsical look we're after. If you drew spirals on the pot, the spiraling foliage will imitate your design. Insert the tallest foliage stem in the center of the arrangement. Insert the shorter foliage stem closer to the edge of the pot. Arrange the foliage and oats so they mix together.

11 INSERT DAISIES

Insert the two tallest daisies in the center, one in front and one in back. Spread the blossoms with your hands. Insert the shorter stems on the left and right and bend the stems.

12) INSERT ACACIA

You'll insert two rings of acacia in this step. Insert the three longest sprigs in a ring around the stems you've already inserted into the center of the foam. Insert the shorter sprigs in a wider ring around the rest of the arrangement. Create depth in the arrangement by staggering the height of the acacia in each ring.

GIVE IT A DIFFERENT LOOK

Use markers to personalize the pot with someone's name for a gift. To make this a primary color arrangement, use red foam on the pot, blue cornflowers and yellow daisies.

Victorian
FOREST

This arrangement brings together the woodsy world of nature and soft pastel colors. It reminds me of a clearing full of soft flowers in the middle of a forest of twigs and branches. Place it in functional rooms, such as the kitchen, dining room or bathroom, to add some interest.

MATERIALS LIST

Silk Flowers
1 walnut branch stem (lime branch or green berry branch also will work)
6 light pink open rose stems
3 pink rosebud stems
5 green celosia stems
5 Queen Anne's lace stems, 3 blossoms per stem
1 variegated button fern stem (Maidenhair fern also will work)

Other Supplies
10" (25cm) low, glass bowl
4" (10cm) green Styrofoam disk
hot glue gun
moss
five 6" (15cm) wooden floral picks
twenty-four 1½" (4cm) ornamental kiwi wedges

CUTTING INSTRUCTIONS

❋ From the walnut branch, cut one 15" (38cm) sprig, one 13" (33cm) sprig and one 11" (28cm) sprig.

❋ Cut one open rose stem to 16" (41cm), one to 14" (36cm), one to 9" (23cm) and the rest to varying lengths between 7" (18cm) and 9" (23cm). Remove any foliage or thorns near the bottom that might keep the roses from entering the Styrofoam cleanly.

❋ Cut one rosebud stem to 11" (28cm) and two to between 8" (20cm) and 9" (23cm).

❋ Cut one celosia stem to measure 13½" (34cm), one to 12" (30cm), one to 9½" (24cm) and two to 8" (20cm). Smooth out the leaves if they are wrinkled.

❋ Cut two Queen Anne's lace stems to 11" (28cm). Cut the individual blossoms off the other three stems so the sprigs measure between 5" (13cm) and 6" (15cm).

❋ Cut five sprigs from the button fern to varying lengths between 5" (13cm) and 8" (20cm).

1 INSERT FOAM DISK

Remove the adhesive backing from the Styrofoam disk and insert it in the center of the bowl. If your disk doesn't have adhesive, glue it down with hot glue. Apply hot glue to the bowl, trying to stay within the area that the Styrofoam will cover.

2 COVER WITH MOSS

Apply hot glue around the sides of the Styrofoam disk. Mold a layer of moss around the disk and apply pressure to make sure it adheres. Remember not to put glue on top of the disk or the flower stems won't go through.

3 SURROUND WITH KIWIS

Place nineteen of the kiwi wedges around the Styrofoam disk. They look best when facing various directions. When you finish the arrangement, you can come back and rearrange the kiwis. You can even glue some in place.

4 INSERT WALNUT BRANCH

Insert the tallest walnut sprig in the center of the foam disk. Insert the two shorter sprigs on opposite sides of the arrangement, both at an angle.

5 INSERT UPPER ROSES

Bend and form the stems before inserting them. Insert the three tallest open rose stems in a triangular arrangement around the center walnut branch. Push them as far into the Styrofoam as possible. They should sit at different heights in the arrangement.

6 INSERT LOWER ROSES

The first three roses created height; now you'll create width. Insert the three shorter open roses in another triangular arrangement around the perimeter of the arrangement. Make this triangular arrangement a bit off center from the last one. Arrangements look more natural if you don't insert one flower directly below another. Insert these roses at lower angles so they face more outward than upward.

7 INSERT ROSEBUDS

Place the tallest bud as close to the center walnut branch as possible, opposite the tallest rose. Bend it to face outward just a bit. Insert the two shorter buds on the side that has only one open rose along the bottom. Bend them to face outward.

8 INSERT TALL CELOSIAS

Insert the tallest celosia stem on one side very close to the center of the arrangement. Insert the two tallest of the remaining stems on the opposite side of center at different angles.

9 INSERT SHORTER CELOSIA

Insert the last two celosia stems on the opposite side (you're back to the side holding the tallest celosia) at more extreme angles, facing more outward.

10 INSERT QUEEN ANNE'S LACE STEMS

Insert one of the Queen Anne's lace stems with three blossoms in the top of the arrangement, slightly off center. Insert the other stem slightly off center to the other side. Spread the blossoms among the other flowers and walnuts to make the arrangement look fuller.

11 INSERT QUEEN ANNE'S LACE SPRIGS

The Queen Anne's lace stems are stiff, so bend them before you put them in the Styrofoam. Insert the sprigs randomly throughout the arrangement, pushing some deeper than others to vary the height. Insert the longest ones near the walnut branches to preserve the general shape of the arrangement.

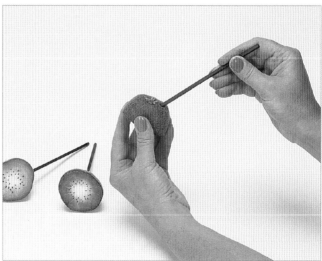

12 PUT FLORAL PICKS IN REMAINING KIWIS

Insert the pointed end of a wooden floral pick into each of the five remaining kiwi wedges at different spots and angles.

13 FILL IN WITH KIWIS

Insert the wedges randomly to fill in the arrangement. Try to push on the picks and not the fruit. Trim some of the picks before you insert them to vary the heights at which the wedges sit.

14 INSERT BUTTON FERN

Insert the button fern sprigs around the perimeter of the arrangement. You may have to push some flowers and leaves aside to get to the Styrofoam. Use the button fern to fill any holes or cover any visible wooden picks. You can even wrap the fern around a pick if necessary.

GIVE IT A DIFFERENT LOOK

Make this a warm arrangement, perfect for fall harvest by filling the bowl with miniature gourds or cranberries. Change the flowers to Fuji mums, sunflowers, black-eyed Susans and button mums.

Vintage
BOUQUET

The soft yet gripping colors really draw you into this arrangement. It's both romantic and welcoming. The colors hint at a strength underneath, but on the surface they're gentle and unassuming. Put the arrangement in a sunroom or other comfortable room where you want to relax and enjoy the coziness of these flowers.

MATERIALS LIST

Silk Flowers
3 blue hydrangea stems with frosted foliage
3 blue lisianthus stems with frosted foliage, 3 flowers and 2 buds per stem
3 pink cabbage rose stems
6 light blue forget-me-not stems
1 frosted lily grass bush with wide blades

Other Supplies
1 green chenille stem
hot glue gun
pen or pencil
9" × 5" (23cm × 13cm) clear, heavy glass vase
double-sided iris wired ribbon, 1½" (4cm) wide
scissors

CUTTING INSTRUCTIONS

* Cut the hydrangea stems to between 20" (51cm) and 22" (56cm).

* Cut the lisianthus to between 20" (51cm) and 24" (61cm).

* Cut the rose stems to between 13" (33cm) and 15" (38cm).

* Cut the forget-me-nots to between 13" (33cm) and 22" (56cm).

* Using scissors, cut two 20" (51cm) grass blades, two 18" (46cm) blades and one 12" (30cm) blade. If the wire inside the grass is too thick, cut it with wire cutters, but use scissors for the rest of the blade to get a clean cut.

* Cut a 6' (2m) length of ribbon.

1 GATHER HYDRANGEAS

Gather the three hydrangea stems in your hand. Hold them loosely and arrange them so they look nice from all sides.

2 ADD LISIANTHUS

Still holding the bouquet in your hand, add the three lisianthus stems around the outside.

3 ADD PINK CABBAGE ROSES

Add the three pink cabbage rose stems also around the outside. Remember to make it look interesting from all sides. As you work, fill out the arrangement by fluffing up the flowers and moving them around.

4 ADD FORGET-ME-NOTS

Loosen your grip as you add more flowers. Add the forget-me-nots throughout the arrangement. As you work, bend some of the rose stems so the forget-me-nots show better.

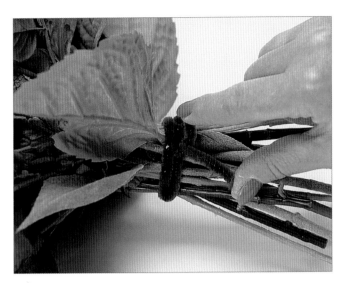

5) TIE TOGETHER WITH CHENILLE STEM

Set the arrangement down. Fluff the leaves and play with the flowers a bit to make sure they lie nicely. Just below the flowers' foliage, wrap a chenille stem twice. Twist the chenille stem to hold it in place.

6) GLUE GRASS BLADES TO BOUQUET

Apply a good amount of hot glue on the flower stems just above the chenille stem. Gather the two longest blades of grass together and place their bases over the glue. It helps to curl the blades around the stems to shape them before actually gluing them down. Hold the blades in place until the glue dries.

7) WRAP BLADES AROUND FLOWER STEMS

Wrap the blades around the group of stems, letting the grass spiral down slightly to cover the chenille stem. Glue the blades in place in the back each time you wrap them around. The last time you wrap them around, glue the blades to the front of the bouquet and let the tips of the grass hang to the side at an angle.

8) WRAP AND GLUE THIRD BLADE

Glue the base of one of the 18" (46cm) blades to the front of the bouquet. Start in the front so the 18" (46cm) blade, which is shorter than those used in the previous step, will end in front. Wrap this blade somewhat loosely in the opposite direction of the first two, gluing it down neatly each time you wrap it around the front.

9   WRAP AND GLUE FOURTH BLADE

Starting in the front again, glue the base of the other 18" (46cm) blade of grass down. Repeat the previous step, wrapping and gluing the blade in the same manner you did the third.

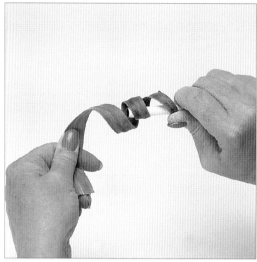

10   FORM SPIRAL FROM SMALLEST BLADE

Form a spiral out of the smallest blade of grass by coiling it around a pen or pencil.

11   GLUE SPIRAL TO BACK OF STEMS

Glue the base of the spiraling blade to the back of the arrangement and wrap it around so the spiral hangs in front. Glue the blade in place in the front as well.

12   FORM RIBBON INTO SPIRAL

Cut the ends of the ribbon at an angle to give them a nice finish. Loop the ribbon loosely around your hand, just as you'd gather a length of rope. Drop it into the vase.

13) ARRANGE THE RIBBON

Separate and spread out the ribbon inside the vase, leaving a hollow space for the stems in the middle. Crinkle the ribbon slightly for an interesting look.

14) PLACE BOUQUET IN VASE

Trim the stems a bit more if desired so the arrangement will sit at a height you like. Hold the vase steady with one hand and insert the stems inside the ribbon with the other. You may need an extra hand to hold the ribbon open. If the arrangement is too heavy and the vase tips easily, trim the stems to make the bouquet shorter, or weigh the vase down with clear marbles.

GIVE IT A DIFFERENT LOOK

By changing the ribbon in the vase you can change the color of the arrangement. Try a textured or patterned ribbon or even raffia. If you use a patterned ribbon, make the arrangement monochromatic.

Chapter Four
NEUTRALS

Neutral colors include creams, buffs, beiges, grays and browns. You won't find these colors in a rainbow, but you will find them abundantly in nature, and isn't natural beauty the most coveted kind? In the world of flower arranging, green also is considered neutral. It's so prevalent in plants and flowers that it goes with just about anything.

Neutrals are the most versatile family of colors. They're uncomplicated, and this simplicity works well in high-traffic areas of your home, such as the foyer or any other busy area where you don't want clutter. Neutrals also act as the perfect backdrop for a rustic, naturally decorated room or a formal, sophisticated wood décor. They blend by adding texture instead of color, but you can make them stand out with striking designs that make use of size or shape.

Pot of
GREENS

Let plants be plants. This all-green arrangement can be as appealing and inviting as a vase of blooming blossoms. Placed in the corner, the arrangement acts as a wonderful accent. Used as a centerpiece, it can breathe life into a room. Plus, it works in any color scheme!

MATERIALS LIST

Silk Flowers

1 variegated large-leaf frosted ivy bush
1 variegated small-leaf frosted ivy bush
1 variegated mauve-green small-leaf ivy bush
1 frosted warnecki bush
1 grapevine branch with green grapes

Other Supplies

5" (13cm) moss green ceramic pot
sheet of Styrofoam
hot glue gun

CUTTING INSTRUCTIONS

* Cut the warnecki bush into 3" (8cm) sprigs.

* Cut the base stem of the grapevine into a 12" (30cm) sprig. From the remaining stems, cut four sprigs about 6" (15cm) long.

1 INSERT FOAM

Turn the pot over and press the opening into the Styrofoam to make an impression. Cut two circles of Styrofoam to this size. Trim one until it will sit in the bottom of the pot. Adhere the Styrofoam circles together with a ring of hot glue around the edges. Glue applied to the top of either circle will prevent stems from entering the Styrofoam smoothly. Drizzle hot glue over the bottom and inside edges of the pot, and drop the Styrofoam in with the smaller circle on the bottom. Apply pressure to make sure it adheres.

2 INSERT LARGE-LEAF IVY BUSH

Insert the large-leaf ivy bush into the center and push it all the way down so the foliage sits directly on top of the Styrofoam. Spread the leaves out in all directions. Some will even hang all the way to the ground.

3 INSERT SMALL-LEAF IVY BUSHES

Insert the small-leaf frosted bush in the front and the mauve-green bush in the back so they sit at the same height as the large-leaf bush. They're smaller, so you won't have to push them in as deep. Mix the different types of ivy together with your fingers to create a pleasing arrangement.

4 INSERT WARNECKI

On a few of the warnecki sprigs, push the leaves almost to the tops of the stems. Insert these in the top of the arrangement, letting the ivy trail down through the arrangement. Insert the rest around the perimeter. Push the sprigs in at different depths to develop variety and interest.

5) INSERT GRAPEVINE

Coil the stems of the grapevine sprigs a bit. Put the tallest sprig in the center. Push it down just a little until the grapes sit at a height you like. Insert the remaining sprigs randomly to fill holes and fill out the arrangement. Avoid letting the grapes sit so far out that they alter the general shape of the arrangement.

GIVE IT A DIFFERENT LOOK

Add some color by changing the color of the container to mauve or purple. Or add dark green foliage in place of the frosted ivy for a winter variation.

Indoor Vegetable
GARDEN

Vegetable and flower gardens can offer as much beauty in fall as in spring, both indoors and outdoors. In a light-colored neutral room, put the arrangement in a noticeable spot so the deep earthy tones capture your attention. In a room with matching tones, the unusual size, shape and texture will catch enough attention on their own.

MATERIALS LIST

Silk Flowers
  6 sarracenia lily stems
  1 seeded eucalyptus stem
  1 green thistle bush
  2 green dogwood stems
  2 blue thistle stems
  2 green celosia (coxcomb also will work)
  7 dracaena stems

Other Supplies
  7" (18cm) square decorative stoneware pot
  8" (20cm) moss-covered Styrofoam ball
  hot glue gun
  3 ornamental succulent cabbage stems
  3 ornamental artichokes

CUTTING INSTRUCTIONS

- Cut the lilies to between 15" (38cm) and 18" (46cm) tall. These are fragile, so be careful when handling them.
- Cut the eucalyptus stem into four sprigs.
- Cut sprigs from the green thistle bush to varying lengths between 8" (20cm) and 10" (25cm).
- Cut the dogwood stems into sprigs measuring between 7" (18cm) and 13" (33cm). Trim excess foliage from the end of each sprig's stem.
- Cut the blue thistle stems into sprigs measuring between 8" (20cm) and 10" (25cm).
- Cut the celosia stems into sprigs measuring between 6" (15cm) and 8" (20cm).

1 GLUE FOAM TO BASE

Cut the Styrofoam ball in half. Don't worry about making a clean cut. Apply a lot of hot glue around the rim of the pot so the uneven edges of the cut Styrofoam will stick. Place the half-sphere over the glue and press down to make sure it adheres.

2 INSERT LILIES

Remove a layer of paper from the bottom inch (3cm) of each lily stem so you'll have a sturdy stem to insert into the Styrofoam. Arrange the six lilies around the center of the Styrofoam, pushing them in about 2" (5cm). You can push the shorter ones in even farther if you'd like to stagger the heights more.

3 INSERT EUCALYPTUS

Insert one eucalyptus sprig into each of the four sides of the Styrofoam just above the rim of the pot, letting them hang down toward the ground. Insert them at different angles to create variety and dimension.

4) INSERT CABBAGES

Insert one cabbage on one side of the lilies and two on the other in a triangular formation. Push the stems all the way in so the cabbages sit right on the ball. Stagger the heights at which you insert them.

5) INSERT ARTICHOKES

Insert the three artichokes between the three cabbages, staggering the heights.

Tip

To insert large stems, such as ornamental cabbages or artichokes, into a strong surface, such as a moss-covered Styrofoam ball, use a knife to make an X in the ball in the spot where you'll insert the stem. Then insert the stem, twisting as you push.

6) INSERT GREEN THISTLE

Push the foliage up the thistle stems a bit. Randomly insert the sprigs close to the center of the ball and the rim of the pot, pushing them in to different depths for variety.

7 INSERT DOGWOOD

Randomly insert the dogwood sprigs throughout the arrangement. If you are having difficulty inserting the sprigs, you may first have to cut an X into the Styrofoam with a knife (see *Tip*, page 97).

8 INSERT BLUE THISTLE

Randomly insert the blue thistle sprigs throughout the arrangement. Put an extra few of the tallest sprigs near the center of the arrangement, sticking up among the lilies.

9 INSERT CELOSIA

Insert the tallest celosia stems near the top of the arrangement. Randomly insert the rest closer to the bottom, filling any holes.

10) INSERT DRACAENA

Add one dracaena stem near the top of the arrangement. This adds another dimension to the arrangement between the tall lilies and the rest of the flowers and vegetables that sit right on the ball. Add the rest of the dracaena stems randomly lower in the arrangement. Push them in as far as possible. Spread the blades and mix them with the other flowers and foliage.

GIVE IT A DIFFERENT LOOK

Change the look of this arrangement easily by replacing the lilies with cattails, branches, corkscrew willow or bamboo. For a splash of color, add red berries or bittersweet.

Copper Cosmos
VASE

These peaches, creams and coppers are considered warm colors, but when you put them together, they blend into a pleasing, quiet, neutral arrangement. The dynamic vertical shape is contemporary, which creates an interesting combination with the old-fashioned colors. This arrangement will work in any neutral- or warm-colored room.

MATERIALS LIST

Silk Flowers
1 white flowering branch
5 magnolia stems
1 burnt orange cosmos stem
1 cream cosmos stem
1 tan cosmos stem
1 orange-pink millet or field wheat stem
1 tan millet or field wheat stem
1 dark green ivy bush

Other Supplies
10" × 4" × 4" (25cm × 10cm × 10cm) copper ceramic vase
sand
8" × 3½" × 3½" (20cm × 9cm × 9cm) Styrofoam vase insert
hot glue gun
moss
scissors

CUTTING INSTRUCTIONS

✳ Cut the flowering branch to leave about 4" (10cm) of the stem below the flowers.

✳ Cut one magnolia stem to 22" (56cm), one to 17" (43cm), one to 15" (38cm) and two to 12" (30cm).

✳ Cut all three cosmos to measure about 18" (46cm) from the tip of the stem to the top of the tallest flower. Trim any foliage off the bottom of the stems.

✳ Cut the orange-pink millet stem to about 19" (48cm).

✳ Cut the tan millet stem to about 16" (41cm).

INSERT FOAM

Fill the vase about a third of the way with sand to weigh it down. Apply hot glue to the sides of the square section of Styrofoam. Also apply a little glue to the rim of the vase. Insert the foam into the vase and apply pressure until the glue dries. The top of the Styrofoam block will sit on top of the rim of the vase.

INSERT FLOWERING BRANCH

Apply hot glue to the sides of the foam. Lay a sheet of moss over it, press down and then trim excess moss with scissors. Insert the flowering branch into the center of the Styrofoam and push it all the way down.

INSERT MAGNOLIAS

Insert the tallest magnolia stem in the center and push it all the way down. Insert the 17" (43cm) stem on the right side and the 15" (38cm) stem just behind the tallest one. Insert one of the shorter stems in the back left corner, facing outward a bit. Insert the other in the front right corner, push it down farther and bend the stem so the blossom faces outward. Insert any leaves left over on the stems.

INSERT COSMOS

Insert each cosmos on a different side of the center and the magnolias. Bend the flowers on each stem a bit so they come out of the arrangement and hang at different angles.

6 **INSERT IVY BUSH**

Bend the short magnolia blossom in the front right corner down a bit and insert the ivy bush in the center so it sits above the magnolia. Pull the ivy branches and flowering branches around and through the arrangement so the leaves and blossoms sit on both sides of center.

5 **INSERT MILLET STEMS**

Insert the orange-pink millet stem in the middle on the left side. Blend it with the other petals. Notice how much it brings out the earth tones of the vase and flowers. Insert the tan millet stem on the right.

Design Tip

Don't worry if your arrangement favors one side or view. It will still be attractive from all angles.

GIVE IT A DIFFERENT LOOK

For a holiday variation, paint the magnolia leaves with copper or gold floral spray paint, and replace the cosmos with red gerbera daisies or poinsettias.

Natural
TEXTURES

The sand and feathers on this clay pot play off aspects of nature and come together with a rich, interesting collection of browns and greens. Feathers, sand and stones bring you outside no matter what the weather. Try this arrangement on a patio or in the foyer.

MATERIALS LIST

Silk Flowers
7 cream-colored field daisy stems, 3 flowers per stem
3 feather cattail stems
2 gold tumbleweed cattail stems
5 brown tumbleweed cattail stems
10 field sunflower stems
1 foliage bush with green berries
1 large maple leaf bush with acorns
3 silver seeded eucalyptus stems

Other Supplies
8" (20cm) round clay pot
strong bond spray adhesive
1 bag of brown decorative stones
1 bag of tan decorative sand
4 bags of 1" (3cm) feathers
2 blocks of dry floral foam
hot glue gun
sand, optional
7 tall pheasant feathers

CUTTING INSTRUCTIONS

❊ Cut the field daisy stems to about 17" (43cm) tall. Trim foliage from the bottom 1" (3cm) to 2" (5cm) so the stems will enter the foam easily.

❊ Cut the feather cattail stems to measure 20" (51cm).

❊ Cut all of the tumbleweed cattail stems to about 17" (43cm).

❊ Cut four field sunflower stems to 14" (36cm). Cut the remaining six to 11" (28cm).

❊ Cut the foliage bush with green berries into four or five sprigs.

❊ Cut the maple leaf bush into 12" (30cm) to 13" (33cm) sprigs.

❊ Cut the eucalyptus stems to about 12" (30cm).

1 COVER POT WITH STONES

Holding the pot from the inside, spray the outside with spray adhesive. Sprinkle decorative stones over the pot.

2 COVER POT WITH SAND

Spray the pot and stones with adhesive, and sprinkle decorative sand over them. The sand should cover the pot and stones to create a nice texture.

Design Tip

If your feathers vary in color, balance their arrangement so that, for instance, you don't have all light feathers on one side and all dark ones on another.

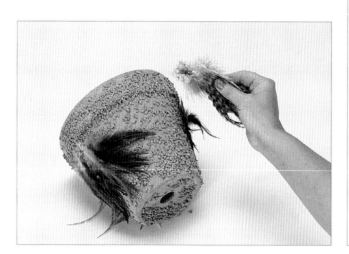

3 COVER POT WITH FEATHERS

Use hot glue to glue a cluster of 1" (3cm) feathers to four sides of the pot so they hang from the bottom of the rim. Leave some space between the clusters so you can see the texture of the pot. Add more glue if necessary to secure the feathers. Once the glue is dry, spread the feathers out. Don't worry if some of the stones fall off when you're working with the feathers.

4 INSERT FOAM BLOCKS

Trim a block of foam to 4" (10cm). Cut another to 7" (18cm) wide and taper it so it will sit snugly in the top of the pot. Apply hot glue around the top edges of the smaller piece of foam and glue the tapered block on top of it. Put hot glue over the bottom and inside edges of the pot, push the blocks to the bottom and hold them while the glue dries. If you'd like to weigh the pot down for stability, fill it with about 4" (10cm) of sand.

5 INSERT DAISIES

Insert one stem of daisies in the center of the pot, and insert the other six stems in a circular arrangement around the center.

6 INSERT FEATHER CATTAILS

Insert the feather cattails in the center of the arrangement. They'll stand slightly taller than the daisies.

7 INSERT TUMBLEWEED CATTAILS

Insert the gold tumbleweed cattails on opposite sides of the center of the arrangement. Then randomly insert the five brown tumbleweed cattails around the outside of the arrangement. Push all of the tumbleweed cattail stems in deeper than you did the daisies so they sit a bit lower.

8 INSERT FIELD SUNFLOWERS

Insert the four tall sunflowers at the top around the center of the arrangement. Insert the six shorter sunflowers randomly around the perimeter at an angle so they face outward.

9 INSERT FOLIAGE WITH GREEN BERRIES

Insert the foliage sprigs around the bottom of the arrangement and push them deep so they cover the foam.

Design Tip

For a more natural look, let the sunflowers around the perimeter hang loosely over the edge of the pot.

10 INSERT MAPLE LEAF SPRIGS

Insert the maple leaf sprigs around the center of the arrangement and bend the stems all the way down so the sprigs hang over the edge of the pot. The maple leaves fill in the base of the arrangement and hide the foam. If you need to cover the foam even more, cut some of the sprigs into smaller, 2" (5cm) lengths.

11) INSERT EUCALYPTUS

Fold the eucalyptus leaves down and insert the sprigs around the center in a triangular arrangement.

12) INSERT PHEASANT FEATHERS

Insert three pheasant feathers in the center, leaning slightly outward. Insert the remaining four feathers about halfway from the top, sticking outward.

GIVE IT A DIFFERENT LOOK

Add color to this arrangement by using colored sand on the pot in orange, red or deep blue. Or take out the sunflowers and replace them with blue delphinium and cornflowers and add a few ostrich feathers.

Chapter Five

SHADES OF BLACK & WHITE

The classic combination of black and white never goes out of style. These shades can stand at the height of sophistication or bend into whimsy and delight. They can evoke a variety of feelings: strength, drama, mystery, simplicity, elegance. They can do all at once or make a simple statement.

Black and white often are perceived as formal colors because they are clean and pure, pristine, exact. But they don't have to be separated from other colors. Every room can use a touch of black or white. Or a black and white room can use a punch of color. To enhance your decorating scheme, use white to create purity and black to ground, or anchor, a room.

Rows of
WHITE

There's not much room for color variation in black-and-white color schemes, so the interest has to come from the design. Many flower arrangements use one or two types of large blossoms and fill the rest of the space with smaller flowers. Here, five types of large blossoms come together to form one uniform section of white. From across the room, you'll notice a simple black tray and a block of white. As you approach, you'll be surprised to discover so much more beautiful detail within the arrangement.

MATERIALS LIST

Silk Flowers
- *1 green ivy garland*
- *4 white open rose stems*
- *4 white field daisy stems with black centers*
- *5 ranunculus stems with black centers*
- *5 white tulip stems*
- *3 white lisianthus stems, 2 flowers and a bud per stem*

Other Supplies
- *3" × 13" × 10" (25cm × 33cm × 8cm) black tray*
- *sheet of Styrofoam*
- *hot glue gun*
- *moss*
- *scissors*
- *greening pins*

CUTTING INSTRUCTIONS
❊ Cut all the flowers to 2½" (6cm) tall.

1 COVER WITH MOSS

Cut a 9½" × 12" (24cm × 30cm) piece of Styrofoam. Apply hot glue all over the bottom of the tray. Drop the Styrofoam into the tray and apply pressure until the glue dries. Run hot glue around the edge of the top of the Styrofoam and cover it with moss. Trim the moss with scissors if necessary. Don't worry if you accidentally trim too much moss. You'll cover the edges in the next step.

2 INSERT A FRAME OF IVY

Secure the ivy garland around the edges of the arrangement with greening pins. Make sure the garland lies completely flat so it doesn't pull up later. Insert the greening pins at an angle for a more secure hold. Trim any extra ivy off the end and tuck it in so the frame looks seamless.

3 INSERT ROSES

Insert the roses in a row on the far left, shorter side of the tray. They all should sit at the same height.

4 INSERT FIELD DAISIES

Insert the daisies in a row next to the roses. Make the row as full as possible and about the same width as the row of roses.

5 INSERT RANUNCULUSES

Insert the ranunculuses in a row next to the daisies.

6 INSERT TULIPS

Insert the tulips in a row next to the ranunculuses. The tulips will sit a bit higher than the other blossoms, so space them out a bit more than you did the other flowers to balance the height.

7 INSERT LISIANTHUS

Place the three tallest lisianthus blooms in the front, back and middle of the last row. Fill in the holes in this row with the last bloom and the lisianthus buds.

GIVE IT A DIFFERENT LOOK

For a holiday variation, use paperwhites, white poinsettias, winterberries, poppies and holly. To add a little color, use filler flowers such as statice or waxflower.

Simple
ELEGANCE

This arrangement is so simple that you don't even need to cut any flowers. And isn't simplicity what the black-and-white color scheme is all about? The black vase provides the most dominant color here, but the white of the blossoms adds some liveliness. The green of the grass is considered neutral in this arrangement, but the way the grass spreads in all directions adds a sense of welcome that would not be present with just black and white. Put these flowers in a larger room where the entire view can be absorbed at once.

MATERIALS LIST

Silk Flowers
1 onion grass bush
4 large white-green anthurium stems
3 small white-green anthurium stems

Other Supplies
12" × 4" (30cm × 10cm) black ceramic vase
sand

CUTTING INSTRUCTIONS

❄ No preparation required!

1) ADD ONION GRASS

Fill the container three quarters with sand. Drop the onion grass bush into the container and spread the grass in all directions. Trim the stem if it is too long for the vase.

2) ADD LARGE ANTHURIUMS

Insert the large anthuriums into the sand, pushing them in at different depths. Bend the stems outward so their staggered heights seem even more obvious.

3) INSERT SMALL ANTHURIUMS

Insert the smaller anthuriums in the center of the arrangement.

4) BEND STEMS

Bend the stems of the smaller anthuriums so the blossoms don't stick straight up. Stagger the height of the smaller anthuriums among each other and the large anthuriums.

GIVE IT A DIFFERENT LOOK

Change the large focal flower to match the season. Use sunflowers in fall, red gerbera daisies in winter and parrot tulips in the spring. Or simply change the mood by using magnolias for a formal look or pincushion protea for something more exotic.

Corkscrew and
DAISIES

The unusual angles and shapes in this arrangement contrast with the simplicity of the colors just as the black contrasts with the white. Contemporary décors call for something a little different, and these flowers serve that purpose whether they sit on the kitchen table, mantelpiece or side table or in the window.

MATERIALS LIST

Silk Flowers
2 white-cream miniature gerbera daisy sprays with black centers
2 corkscrew willow branches

Other Supplies
black spray paint
10" (25cm) tall crystal vase
3 bags of black and white marbles

CUTTING INSTRUCTIONS

✳ Cut the daisy stems to measure 17" (43cm).

✳ Cut one corkscrew willow branch to 26" (66cm). Cut two 22" (56cm) sprigs from the other branch.

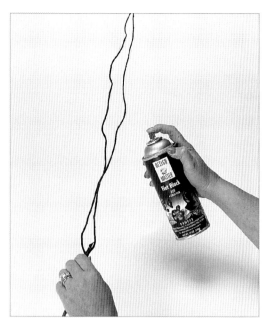

1   PAINT CORKSCREW WILLOW

Spray paint the willow branches black. Set them aside to dry. Don't worry about covering the very bottom tips of the branches with paint. They'll be hidden by the marbles.

2   ADD MARBLES

Fill the vase almost to the top with the black and white marbles.

3   ADD DAISIES

Insert the daisy sprays into the vase. Leave one spray fairly straight. Bend and shape the flowers of the other spray with your hands to make fun angles and give the arrangement a contemporary feel.

4   ADD CORKSCREW WILLOW BRANCH

Insert the tallest willow branch in the center of the arrangement.

5) ADD CORKSCREW WILLOW SPRIGS

Insert the two shorter willow branch sprigs on either side of the center to soften the arrangement a bit.

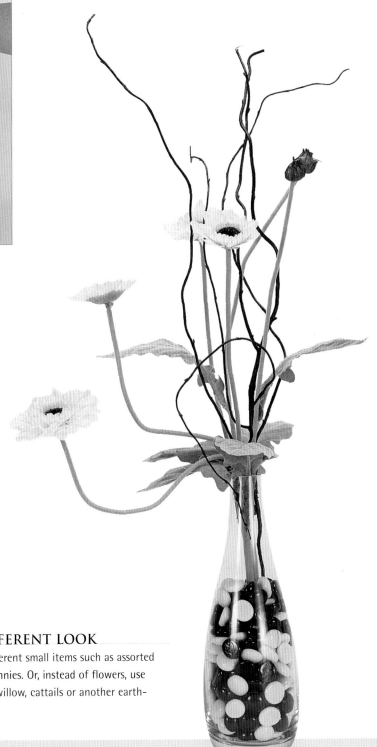

GIVE IT A DIFFERENT LOOK

Fill the vase with different small items such as assorted buttons or copper pennies. Or, instead of flowers, use branches, corkscrew willow, cattails or another earth-toned foliage.

Resources

In addition to the mail-order and online resources listed here, check your local craft and floral supply shops for general floral tools and supplies. Purchase fine silk flowers from your local craft stores or your florist. If you have trouble finding some materials, you can purchase them through my web site.

Mariemont Florist
7257 Wooster Pike
Cincinnati, OH 45227
(800) 437-3567
www.mariemontflorist.com
to contact the author, gather general information or assistance or purchase materials used in this book

OTHER U.S. RESOURCES

Dick Blick Art Materials
P.O. Box 1267
Galesburg, IL 61402
(800) 828-4548
www.dickblick.com
for general art and craft supplies

Save-On-Crafts
100 Cotton Lane
Soquel, CA 95073
(831) 475-2954
(831) 475-1801
www.save-on-crafts.com
for floral wire, foam, adhesives, tape, raffia, moss and silk flowers

Silk Flowers Express
3467 Rutrough Road
Roanoke, VA 24014
www.silkflowersexpress.com
for silk flowers

Index

The best in **creative instruction and inspiration** is from North Light Books!

Venture down the path o' craft with the artistic inspiration in *Wild with a Glue Gun*! Whether you want to start your own craft club or you're an avid member seeking new and fun projects, you'll enjoy making any of the 75 crafts found in this book, including a miniature serenity garden, sparkling origami lights, darling charm bracelets and more! You'll also find resources for creating your own craft club. So get crafty with your friends, and share the joy of creating!

ISBN 1-58180-472-5, paperback, 144 pages, #32740-K

Here are 20 beautiful wreath projects, perfect for brightening up a doorway or celebrating a special time of year. You'll find a range of sizes and styles, utilizing a variety of creative materials, including dried herbs, sea shells, cinnamon sticks, silk flowers, autumn leaves, Christmas candy and more. Clear step-by-step instructions ensure beautiful, long lasting results every time!

ISBN 1-58180-239-0, paperback, 144 pages, #32015-K

Capture the essence of the seasons with these simple, stunning floral arrangements. With a few basic techniques, a handful of materials, and a little creativity, you can make eye-pleasing accents for every room in your home. All the flower arranging advice you need is inside, plus 15 projects using silk flowers, greenery, leaves, pinecones, gourds and more.

ISBN 1-58180-108-4, paperback, 96 pages, #31810-K

Make your holidays brighter and more special by fashioning your very own floral décor! Cele Kahle shows you how to create a variety of gorgeous arrangements, swags, topiaries, wreaths and even bows. With 19 creative projects, clear step-by-step guidelines, beautiful full-color photos, and Cele's advice and instruction, you'll make every holiday more special—even if you have little or no experience.

ISBN 1-58180-259-5, paperback, 128 pages, #32124-K